DORO
LASK

THEA
Y

THE
SHIN

ING

Wave Books / Seattle & New York

Published by Wave Books

www.wavepoetry.com

Copyright © 2023 by Dorothea Lasky
Wave Books titles are distributed to the trade by

Consortium Book Sales and Distribution

Phone: 800-283-3572 / SAN 631-760X

Library of Congress Cataloging-in-Publication Data

Names: Lasky, Dorothea, 1978– author.

Title: The shining / Dorothea Lasky.

Description: First Edition. | Seattle : Wave Books, [2023]

Identifiers: LCCN 2023009926 | ISBN 9781950268856 (paperback)

Subjects: LCGFT: Poetry.

Classification: LCC PS3612.A858 S55 2023 | DDC 811/.6–dc23/eng/20230303

LC record available at https://lccn.loc.gov/2023009926

This book is also available in limited edition hardcover (ISBN 9781950268917)

Designed by Crisis

Printed in the United States of America

9 8 7 6 5 4 3 2 1

First Edition

Wave Books 111

The objects see me as I see them. —Paul Valéry

THE SHINING

SELF-PORTRAIT

IN THE HOTEL

I am here by myself
And I have finished everything
There are no pretensions
No way around the door
I have eaten all the cans of beans and lemons
And am face drunk on the floor
There are no cats here
Only children
Crawling around above me
Yes, they look at me
They absolutely do not know me
They want to look at me
And tell me they know
They are fed and ready for the ceremony
I haven't prepared anything
I am so wholly unprepared for this
I was told I'd have a lifetime
Now the whole thing is coming at me
I can't even see myself in the mirror

Or in the space between the mirror and the wall
He brings me to the grey fixtures
And mentions that we are dead
Who didn't know that
When I checked into this
Godforsaken hellhole
They locked me in the tiny yellow room
With no belongings but my lipstick
And said that I'd be ok as long as I didn't make
A movement
In and out he entered me
Letting me know what I could or could not say
I wasn't saying anything
I never wanted to say a thing
I only wanted to see myself as vast and unknowable
In some horrific ocean
Instead they drove me for hours
And up on the lands I wandered
Red boots and a dark-brown coat
I collected aqua pencils, four of them
They said it's your job now to tell this story
But I was no storyteller
I was an action figure that had no set box
I was tied up inside the cardboard
A little person took me down
And drooled all over me

I was not a seer at all
And they knew it
I was only her
And will be forever
And when you see her empty eyes
That's me
Except my eyes are gleaming
And when there are tears
I will cry them
Only for the days that have left me
They drove me here and locked me in
A tiny yellow room
They said to be quiet
But I am not able
To be quiet
Any longer

POETRY HATES YOU TOO

A light falls on the bitter afternoon
That half sounds like a jetliner taking off
Or sounds like all of those unfairly dismissed
To their perfectly absurd little rooms for all eternity
But I won't dedicate this poem to them
Because the real and feminized world was made for
Their sweet countenances
Which upturn at the sight of the falling light
Which speak of nights spent in a dream
No instead I dedicate this poem
Dead and useless as it is
To the man who sits at his wooden desk
Constructing the annals
Of that conservative leaflet
No one would die for
Strumming his computer keys
Like the way he fumbles with a clitoris
Or who sits in an expansive city lawn with that pretty girl
Hoping his particulars won't find him
Dribbling his expensive gin all over her reddening dress
This is a love poem for that man

That one who bemoans us plebeians
Who value the wide swath of time
That we find ourselves in
Rather than value the academic study
Of poems that denounce emotion or real feeling
For as he sits unbuttoning a pair of purpled slacks
He will find me there eventually
Sitting with the both of them
My arm around them in the photo
Sharing a seat with them in the cab ride
While he pontificates about his money or his status
Once he reads again into the poem
That he so wildly admires
He will find me there too
Rising from the bath
Body decaying within the stanzas
That he so loves but couldn't see fit
To publish in its own time
He may find me too
As he is taking down that tattered book
While sitting by the fire
In search of what words once moved him
And with drowsy eyes finds this poem instead
Staring back at him
With words of immense caution
To be careful of the poems you preach

Poetry I too dislike it
But I dislike him more
And I will write it until they take it
Away from me
If it means I can speak
What he never will
In defense of it
Poetry I hate you too
But little man
I hate you more
So sweet upturned faces to the sun
Make the poems be the things you give everyone
They must carry on

STRANGE HUMOR

The key to surviving in here
Is to pretend every room is haunted
Even when it isn't
All these old buildings
Everything still lives here

For years I have woken
In the middle of the night
Knowing that she sits there
Yes she's looking at me
Yes she has something to say

She never does though
All these old buildings
Thick against the day sky
The key to surviving here
Is to pretend each moment is haunted

All these old buildings
Are thick domes
Against the night sky

So I took a picture
I took a picture of them

While we were walking
Under layers of fruit and flowers
All these old buildings
Somehow I know she's still watching
She still has something to say

A LION

In the bedroom
After fainting
The therapist comes in

In the bed a stuffed lion
Who sits behind the boy
In utter repose

I think that I have found
The way back in
Although I am not quite there yet

You could have picked anyone
I chose to see the inner life
It was orange, cream, and beating

HIGH CEILINGS

It's this or that
But it's pretty much art
The way the rug is on the ground
So anxiously

The music so abstractly
Entering the space
Where I can meet anyone
Except you

Now I am counting the words
That are said
To make sure
It is I who say them

I am bent over the mirror
The way that they bend over a lake
In the picture of the maze
I'm smiling

OLD PHOTO

It says 1921 in the picture
And I am smiling
But it's not me anymore
Or maybe it never was

He gets so angry when he is drunk
And throws the baby across the room
I get so angry when I am ready
I throw myself into oblivion

It says 1999 in the picture
I am wearing a purple dress
There are great planets circling
And ahead of me

I never asked for this to be my name
He put a set of pictures up on the wooden wall
He said: Find yourself
But that part was easy

FOOD COURT

It's a perfect temperature in here
And everything is clean
Except the souls

When you open the cabinets
There's every can imaginable
Rows and rows of tomatoes

They ask me to make them
Bread and eggs
But all that I can see

Are cans and yellow trays
Everyone starts singing
Including the hungry

My soul is as clean
As the refrigerated walls
And I tell them all so

Suddenly eggs appear
I crack each one
Into a yellow tray

You know I love
A tortured love story
But this isn't what I planned for

In the middle of the accident
I crack another egg
On the head of a disbeliever

Everything is perfectly adequate
I stir my lukewarm cereal
My soul is as clean as the spring

I tell no one that
Because no one ever listened
I crack an egg into the air

It drops like an accident
Because no one ever loved it
I say to no one at all

You know I love a tortured story
I think to write it down
Instead I crack this egg

Here for you
So don't be sorry
Just take the lukewarm pudding

And think of me
I'm all alone here
Maybe for forever

I crack this lukewarm story
Into your bowl
And you sop it up

I know you love a love story
You sop up my blood pudding
With my head

THE GOLD BALLROOM

A dress that is high in the neck
Is best to see yourself in

I have come here from far away
To see what time could do to me

Everywhere there is the woman
Slouched over her drink

In the season of despair
As it's always nighttime here

Or should I say, there's always a becoming
I lay my life in front of you without cause

And you take stock of it
Deem it not worthy

I was always the right person
To medicate danger

I take out my little metal purse
So many vials in exactitude

So many moments
Where the past was left waiting

I take out my tiny succulent angels
If you won't have me

Will you at least try them
They've been in their jars

For all eternity
Surely something could come out of it

And if not, let's glide across this carpet
You and I, so gracefully

What you don't know in story
I'll give to you in action

I take out my tiny new beginning
And ask you to think again

Maybe this time will be different
I glide you across the carpet

That is pink and gold
And you must admit

The swirl of time
Provides us an opening

You take stock of my life
And deem it wholly acceptable

I take out my tiny book
And read you these words

And even you must admit
There was always something there

There was always something there
That was waiting

TIME

When I was brought here
It looked just like the mountains
But it wasn't
It was my life

Eat eat you little vermin
And this is probably bad karma
There goes the calendar
A kind of predator

Legs in sneakers
Like knives
Because I am way stronger
Than I ever thought I was

I was Dorothea Lasky
Now my name is nothing
But I never forgot my name
Did you

JEANS

They have got me in a car
I am a little rough and tumble
Nevermind, I'm trouble
And I take a rough ride
Whenever you put me there
Or I really don't care
About your perversions or necessities
I am not excessive but I'm true
There is a strange music
From the old days
That they play in this room
I am not in there
I am locked in the bedroom
Everyone else can see me
All I see is the wall
It is pink and floral
Dumb white flowers
Hanging over in the surprise garden
I remember a day with heat
In fact I remember everything very nicely
He went home after a short conversation

Or really it was hours of us laughing
If I could go back there
I think he'd still remember me
I think he'd say
That I was there
Hours and hours of us laughing
I think he'd say that we were there
In that wretched garden
Where I found everything
Hours and hours
And when it was all over
He and I
We were still there
We were still waiting
Hours and hours of laughing
And when you really look
You must admit
There was always something there
Something there
That was waiting

THE TRUMPET

Nature calls
But this isn't natural
I am pushing a cart all along the hallways
On it is a plate with toast
A stack of butter falling to the side
In the glass milk still powdered sifting

I am watching everything around me
But also my head is forcefully to the side
In my low mind
A kind of question
Where is everyone
And why

Long ago as a child
I liked to dream of what might happen
I never expected this sort of thing
I only wanted love and magic
This part is a fairy tale
But only the ending of one

MARRIAGE

I am a very paranoid and awful person
Dragging my knee behind me like a large curse
Ten minutes before
Meeting someone important
I pretend to know the answer that I so clearly don't

Shuffling my papers together
In a huff
A great hearing of a great accord
Expecting the worst
And meeting something even worse

What is language
Is the question I ask the large peacock
Who sits at the end of the bed
Smiling the grin of demons
Bending its neck to get a good look at me

Oh I'm a monster too
And a reticent one
I'll spend the rest of my days on the sofa
But my love I'll give you the chair
There, There

BLUE CHRISTMAS

I am so excited
I am dancing with my sister
In the front of the restaurant
Two men look at us and sniffle

We are wearing the clearest blue dresses
That look like the sky in the middle of the spring
There is a pretend antagonism to our song
But we know that we really love each other

Years later they will film us as children
Wearing matching dresses again
But the blue will be muted
Soon after they will show us chopped up

As always they will be obsessed
With the violence men can do to us
But I was only ever trying to do my job
I only ever wanted to be a movie star

OLD TV

I don't ask questions anymore
I am almost done with it
They have left me sandwiches
Or more so white bread
With marshmallow fluff

We talk of the same things
And I am almost always tired of it
I don't have any questions
To ask now, only sadness
I am almost over all of this

But when I stare into that caustic set
I can see myself and also you
I love you, don't you know that
I thought I made it obvious
But also I cloaked it in a dream

When the show is over I'll wake up
Tighten my robe

And will wheel the TV into the basement
Maybe after I'll stop in the kitchen for a cup of mint tea
Won't you join me

No wash your filthy hands
And meet me in the square room
I'll carry this cup and saucer for two
You know I can carry us to the boundary
Look inside yourself, I'm still waiting

TWINS

Man in an Easter suit
Leans into me
To kiss me

But I am not in the mood for that
I turn and cough
I am desirable

I exhaust myself
On ways to find out
How to do the work I'm meant to do

In the room
Two girls
They look at me

They say:
We acknowledge you
And, Hello there

I was a rose girl always
They doused me with fire perfumes
And put me in a blue bag

I am not in the mood
For anything
I leak desire

I owe this all to poetry
Strange humor
I found you again

HUNGER

I was starving but I didn't dare eat
I just sat there waiting for dinnertime
So someone could cut me
A few apple slices
I had spent my whole life
Feeling this way again

The table was long and wooden
Instead of friends there
It was completely empty
Except for the spirits
And a long green tablecloth
With candles of different dimensions

I hunger for you now
Do you find that strange
That I squandered all those years with you
Now I'm stuck here forever
At least I can write my way out of it
At least my vocabulary can still do this to me

THE MIRROR

I am prepared to be everything
I was always much more
Than I gave myself credit for
I still am
Looking upon this surface
As smooth as a lake
Where I see the sister of myself
In the same blue dress
I am no longer who she was
But I am better maybe
More fully realized
The days have passed
As they say
I have let out so many loves
And let out
My heart to too many
I've been everything
They asked me to be and more
And yet I didn't yield at all
I only just gave them my entire soul
Walking throughout this place
Even they can't help how lonely

Everything is
How utterly empty this place is
How lonely it is to love anything
I love poetry
And in every way
This smites me
Poetry with no roots
In the soil
Just wrenched free by wind
I walk in a blue bathrobe
Pushing the cart full of eggs
Back to the kitchen
No one ever talks too much
About the part where
The dishes need to be cleaned
Where are the poems about
Someone wiping clean
Over and over again
The eggs falling somewhere
The same white plates
I want to read that poem maybe
I want to be the water in the drain
That for a moment
Is connected to the moment
And then quickly
Is set free

Or the refuse
I want to be the residue that they bag up
And bring to the incinerator
That they are so quick to shut out
And that when burning
Changes the air
They asked for me
Then when I appeared here
Slick as a surface
On the bottom of the ocean
They threw a rock at my sister
And asked for another mother
Well it's too late
I intend to do this for a while
There are still days
And nights
There is still the late afternoon
Where I am so wholly alone
The place is emptied out
I am so entirely upended
From anything I know
And yet I could do this forever
Walking back and forth
With this cart of eggs
And I will keep doing it
No I do intend to

RED AIRPLANE

I am surrounded by light
In the middle of the morning
We are going somewhere
Back to the West
I had only known what palm trees
Looked like and now here I am again
There is snow but it's not cold
In fact I am so warm in this place
The red velvet interior
Making a home of me
I have almost gotten this far before
Now I look again at the time
We will land in no way ever
Everything is stuck here
I could write a letter or worse yet
I could keep looking off into the distance
No one knows my name in the land of ecstasy
It's spring again and no one knows my name still

VISION

I am staring off
When I should be working
I am having an idea
Of something very far away from here

I should be working
Instead I sit here dreaming
With my face in a scowl
I can see you in the next room

I can even see myself
Backward and forward
Pink rocket
That sputters into destiny

I am standing here
Above the green maze
And the little children
Having an idea of something

Could it be you and me
Oh but those dreams died long ago
You should know
You killed them

RUGS

I love the way that the purple and green
Go up the steps to where she is
And all you see
Are these undulating phalluses
And little spots of semen
Where I left them

Of course there is that red and orange
And black, all done up
Like a honeycomb
They say that the rocketships live there
Or maybe the bees
They say that there's life there

And don't forget all the rugs
With the images we have stolen
They are maybe the most prominent
They have graphic patterns
Orange and purple
Triangular phalluses

There's something special though
About the ones that they hung up
There they put the warriors
The people who fought us
We hang their faces up there like objects
Then in the middle of the night

We take them down
We step on them
Don't forget about the grass
Ringing the outside
I ran through it, soft green weave
When it was all over, I slept there

SWIMMING POOL

There are more important things
Than physical force
But still you probably
Don't want to piss me off

I have definitely applied
Turquoise eye shadow
Glittery and clear coated
In the middle of winter

I don't exist at all
They didn't even make me
They saved every sex scene
For a weird green bathroom

Still I know somewhere
I'm important
As the music slows
I ascend from the gloomy waters

MAN IN THE WINDOW

Man out the window is looking at me
Man in the hallway is coming near me
Man is standing over the bed watching
When I wake up man says good morning
But I don't hear him
Instead I am considering the nature
Of what is beautiful
Man in the corner is spitting on the floor
He says my name and then takes it for his own
Man is saying that he wrote this poem
Man in the center of the stage
Tells everyone that we know each other
When I am dead man makes a speech
About how well we knew each other
He says we were best friends
And in some ways, we were

RED RUM

Lipstick is one of the very finest elixirs
It has a soft consistency
And can write on glass
Red rum is sweet
And candied
With cherries from the
Bottom of the bottle
We sip it so gracefully
I am in love again
His name is something
But who can remember
Memory is a lake
And all of that
I can't remember
Where I left my last exercise
I was only ever sitting here
Watching the neon burn out
I have taken my red lipstick
And written Help across my chest
He looks at it so kindly
I know I am real again

I can feel the sweet bitters
Of the drink make me into a woman
I am not crying
I am writing sonnets in my mind
About all of the vacations
We will take after this one
I throw the glass against the wall
The only thing that matters in love is passion

MAZE

I was always
Just a little lady
But I am sick of pretending
You actually know
What you're talking about
We go around and around and say nothing
We do this for so many years
It's sunny outside for most of it
But we do not go out there
We stay inside
The more people that come into the house
The lonelier we feel
Of course they don't understand artists
And you are one
You definitely know the rhythm of language
Put into squares
And then funneled out a little conveyor belt
You love excising the drama from anything
I listen greedily
But it makes me very bad
It's like eating worms

That have already eaten my body
You feed them to me like candy
You stuff them into my mouth
As you are talking
Knocking me over
And trying to enter me
And then one day
I go outside
I run around the grassy puzzle
I try to make sense of what is glistening
You stand over it
In my dreams and elsewhere
You are as big as any devil
You look with your eyes on me
And I am both flattered
And also flattened
I had no chance here
I was only always the little lady
You were more than that
You held the grand design

PERFUME

Pink flamingos meet in the head
There was one rose and one violet
I kept them so close to me

On the tabletop
A sense of confusion
But I couldn't stop it, I permitted

I let in the odor of another rose
Melting into a peony
I murdered the hydrangea into tiny petals

A vocabulary of bears
I crouched down
There were so many flowers

In the space of the garden
I ordered each mouthless opening
Until they formed into spirit mouths

Birth and death
Are not the same thing
Every pretty floral is painted

On the wall, a key to the whole thing
I pressed it and the walls turned around
There was wallpaper everywhere
It smelled just like the wilderness

BLUE HALLWAY

I am going up the steps
With a knife
I am scared and looking around

I feel everything so acutely
Despite the lack of acute attention
My husband is trying to kill me

I am trying to outsmart him
But all around me are the ghosts
I turn my head and see a bear and a man

This isn't at all the way I imagined it
I have learned not to imagine anything
I keep running with the knife

I go into my little apartment and lock the door
It's no use because the ghosts are here too
Outside the window it is radioactive

In fact I can't even begin to tell you
How scared I am to go out there again
I sit on my bed and look at the mirror

There is a refrigerator
I could eat something
Instead I get a glass of water

I decide that actually now is the time to dance
I call up a song on the radio
I request it with my mind

Now for effect I am turning and turning
No one can see me
Then I invite them all in

All the people I was running from
Are here now
I am in the place I have dreamt about

I am in the space
That has kept me up every night
Even my brother is finally here

We are having a party
I get out the cut cheese and meat logs
People discuss their hair

I have hairy legs
From so many months indoors
I've always liked everything furry

I get out my paint collection
Now it's time for art class
I get out my clean brushes

Everyone sits down and I say hush
My son and husband are here
They are so proud of me

I discuss the effects of line on paper
And the ways in which form is everything
I use a tiny pencil to outline the edges

I am painting an orange
Suddenly someone gasps
"An orange is genius!"

Then I start crying and crying
I've always secretly known
That I was a genius

I was just waiting for this moment
All my life I was just waiting
To be in this hell here

And to be called a genius
I pretend to act demure
And bat my heavy eyelashes

My husband says:
"Oh I knew that she was a genius
From the moment I laid eyes on her"

He hands me a dry martini
I take a drink
This is my night after all

THE BEAR

The poem is gone forever
But I was made for this

I am crouched between a man's thighs
Where only the body lay

The poem is lost forever
Completely upended in its lettering

I am in a fur suit
Looking different completely

No one ever told me
I had to save you

In every goodbye
There is a poem that is gone now

Watch out—
Timber!

In every single hello
There is a bleeding hell

SNOW MAZE

Everything feels cold
I'd love a little warmth
But I am stuck out here
While they warm themselves
By the fireplace or by the fire
They have no bones
And are completely ash
I am not I am still flesh
I am stuck somewhere
In the corner of the maze
No one can find me
But I am speaking so loudly
The real life is a dream
I woke up so many times
They thought I was still dead
My arms are frozen
And I can feel the pain in my arms
They say if you can still feel pain
That means that you are living
Trauma has always been a part of my poetics
I have been writing this poem

For my entire life

What is this curtain of flesh

On the bed of our desire

I meant it when I said I loved her

Snow

Snow

A LOVELY WORLD

I am walking through the hotel
Every time I am so sad
That I want to die

It's a place where I can keep
Everything I've never been
Brave enough to get to

Poets have moons and money
To get themselves through
The longest night imaginable

But I've had these rooms
To beckon me
With their own brand of patience

The warmest rose emanates
From the hall near my bedroom
I'll enter if you will

I know that in this world
I will always be waiting
But you let go of life, with a thud

Instead I waited for you
Hiding here in plain sight
Like a flower

THE AX

He told me violence
Doesn't exist
So I hefted him up the stairs
While he was dreaming

He told me that how I saw it
Was not so much how it went
And that I must have hit
My head while singing

He repeated something
About exhaustion
Yes, I was tired
Of dusting the finery

Something else opened up
When he sat himself
Down on me
And cried

It was still beautiful
Every last moment
Of this completely
Inappropriate love

He insisted the violence
Was just something I had imagined
I got lost running away
Finally it happened

THE GREEN MAZE

All the artists of the world
Are my brothers and sisters
Even as I am locked in this house
Of the high ceilings and slanted bookcases
With all of the charlatans and naysayers
The soupy packagers and droopy preachers
Pushing me down a ditch
Or through the open window
To an indefinable snow hill
Where I will surely not survive it
I still call on my family
To know what's real or not
And whatever they say
To you chasing you down
A hallway that will be forever estranged
Be who you are
It is your job
To carry it on
No matter what bull is chasing you
For a hundred years with an ax
In the green landscape of your dreams

Live your dreams

And push through

Until it is daybreak and you see the sun

Begging you to find the new space to go on

After all it was and always will be

Your job

To go free

So protect the things that are worth preserving

That's partially you too

Protect those upturned faces

Into the sun

No matter what

They must carry on

AFTER THE PARTY

After the party
There will be balloons
Strewn across the hallway
You will think
What's he doing out there
Dressed like the enemy
And why does he look
So happy
But that's because you
Won't be happy at all

We took things
Way too far
Last night
But I always do
Take things way too far
But so do you too
We are the dumbest animals
In our sick lakes
And after all of this is over
We will just be empty again

Red and yellow are strewn
Across the lakes of
The shiny floor
And when I go to pick
Some of it up
I am told it's not my job anyway
Along will come the bitter nightman
He always takes things
Way too far
But then I do too

What's he doing here
Dressed like the enemy
I see his costume
We have slept in our
Sequined coffins
Why is he always there
To taunt me
Looking like
He's so happy
About it

Live or die
By the light
Of old balloons
Why do I look

So happy about it
Maybe because
After all of this is over
I'll just be empty again
Dressed like the enemy
With my red guitar

Ready to play another round
Why when you take
Things so far
Are you so happy about it
I ask the nightman
Who are these flowers even for
He said they were for you
Why are you dressed like the enemy
And when I'm done with you
You'll just be empty again

FRAMED PICTURES

At the very last moment
It is morning
Nothing is redemptive
About it
There's a buffet breakfast somewhere
That no one cares about
It's the next day
After hours of sex in the garden
We are walking across the golden walkway
A lion is running
He shouts that the green city is near
But something else propels us
Not the stale brown liquid
Or rubbery proteins
But the overflowing sugar of memory
That these objects hold
Across the golden path
21 pictures wait for you
You will keep walking til you see
The one you were destined for
People think this is all an accident

They think life could happen to anyone
When you see it you will be drawn
To the image of yourself
In that forgotten year
His face being watered down
By the elements for too many moments
He will be smiling at a party
And you will recognize what he's saying
The dead only speak through poetry
So make the poems be the things
That you give everything
They must carry on

CLOSING SCENE

I buy a floral dress and grumble
I am holding an ax
No one can hear me
Because no one is around
I am screaming in some respects
But it sounds just like frost
I have tried to kill so many people
I wasn't even in the right arena
I tried to kill you
But who wanted to
So you should go on and live
Take the snowcat and drive
Drive so far away from here
With the boy, who will always be broken
I'll stumble
You hurt my leg with your hormones
I'll stumble then fall over
My heart is cold
It always has been
I will sit down for a rest
I can see in my mind my mother

Setting the table for supper
She is glowing with a watery aura
I am so thirsty for fire
I am now starting to fight it
I understand that this is all for me
You are running through the snow
You have the child with you
You aren't scared
You know this is the part of the story
Where you go free

GOING THROUGH
A MOUNTAIN

When the ghosts came after me
I just thought about the night sky
The way it twists and bends
And still maintains its picture
Of a lion, a goat, a peacock
How we name our very sacred
After the patterns it brings

Doesn't everyone feel
There's an order to things
I asked the landscape
Instead it answered: Chaos

How hard it is to accept
That even the skyline
Doesn't feel anything
Like an order at all

Icky lousy horrible dread
Is what I feel every day of my life
So I wrote a book so scary
It would mimic real life
In all the worst ways

After all I only remember
The hospital bed
Where they both lay dreaming
Both of my parents
It could have been 2045
It could have been 1408
But it was Room 237
Through and through

After all it was a mountain
I was going through
Where memory is not a literal thing
But a labyrinth
It only coats
When it is able

Where it is so cold outside
In the screaming bedroom
Where it is 4 am always
And you go at it alone

Forgetting for those moments who you are
Or why you even came here
Wandering inside the locked-down hallway
Popping a pill or two
To forget about consciousness

Dear reader I know you are tired too
So maybe you should take another drink
And close down the receptors
Maybe if you're lucky
Someone will give you one
And tell you about your nice eyes
Maybe all you need is one good night

One good night of something
And when they rise in the daylight
Tricking us all into morning
Beyond a love of paternalism
Or the patriarchy, or whatever it is
These pink things mean
Except our own self-hatred
Because all we are
Are mirrors of ourselves

Or maybe you should just
Take another drink, Ben Ben

And oh it sucks about your kids, Valentine
Have another little run in the forest
Little blue eyes
Don't worry about the kids
I'm sure their father
Will take very good care of them
When you're gone

I myself was just trying to go there
But instead I saw him walking
In two different directions
But he was one person
My mirror multiplying us like a demon
My demon saying stop now
But it's just you and me, Valentine
We should have loved them better
I know

And one two times
Did I hear the screaming
You know you hear it too
There is no rising into a violet sleep
And walking the day into the trees
Or taking a lemon cocktail
Out on the veranda
In the suite of our youth

With the orange trees
Three trees, three lives
The earth was already dying by then

No he was always there waiting
So masterful
Downstairs in the house
That doesn't exist
Down down way down
When the woman in the tower
She said, Look out!

She was going through a mountain too
When you know
She should have gone
Over it
But I was always vigilant
I was always waiting
So have another drink, Ben Ben
You'll get to me eventually
Don't worry, my dear
I'll wait

And when you finally
Get to the bottom of the glass
You'll find me

That terrible terror of being
That's me

And when you finally get to me
Oh I will be so patient
Have another little toast of something, my children
Real things are lit by the moon
Be a moon, Valentine
Take a little toast of something
I'll just be sitting by the bed
No really
I'll wait for you
I'll wait

ACKNOWLEDGMENTS

Thank you to my family and friends for their endless support. Thank you to Joshua Beckman and everyone at Wave Books for making this book possible. Thank you to the editors of *The Paris Review*, *Poetry*, *The Nation*, *The American Poetry Review*, and *Lana Turner* for originally publishing some of these poems.